Children Growing Funny

A Collection of Poems and Quotes

Kevin Clark

PublishAmerica
Baltimore

First printing

ISBN: 1-4137-4712-4
PUBLISHED BY PUBLISHAMERICA, LLLP
www.publishamerica.com
Baltimore

Printed in the United States of America

I'd like to dedicate this book to children everywhere, with a special thought for those children who experienced the Holocaust. May there be a special place in Heaven for all children who have suffered on this Earth.

A collection of poems, thoughts, and quotes has lived inside of me since the birth of my two sons, Casey and Corey. As I've watched them grow, I am filled with a bitter happiness, as each day they grow I know they take another step closer to being on their own. My own selfishness wants to forever hold onto their small hands and their wide eyes of wonderment. I want to always be their hero, their teacher, their joy, and the daddy who sees their eyes light up when I come into their room. As parents, we know we'll always hold a special place in our own children's hearts, but not like the place we hold during their years of innocence—the years when the sky is the bluest blue and the stars the brightest bright; the years when each new step taken is a step which anxiously waits our approval; the years when fairytales, cartoons, nature, pain, pleasure, excitement and life are all interwoven into each and every new day the moment their eyes open from peaceful dreams; the years we hold onto through photos, poems, thoughts and quotes, such as these.

A Child's Magic

It's in the eyes, that place of dreams,
of long agos and in betweens.
Of never-never land and flights without wings,
of once upon a time, wonderful things.
Like castles and magic and ice cream for lunch.
Like rainbows and melodies sung to a lollipop's crunch.
I once wondered where that place could be,
before you were born, before I could see.
Now it's near and now I know
where all the elves and fairies go.
They dance in your eyes so bright and so clear.
Oh, Son, you have eased my very worst fear
by helping me find that place so dear.
That place I hold in my arms so tight
and place into bed with a soft kiss goodnight.

I remember seeing both of my sons' faces for the first time on the day they were born. I was overwhelmed with emotion each birth. My first son, Casey, was delivered and handed to me after being wiped off, and looked like an angel. He was plump with rosy cheeks and pout lips. I held him in my arms while thinking to myself, that had I picked a child to be mine from all of the millions in the world, this is whom I would have picked. When my second son, Corey, entered this world, my wife, Patricia, had a much more difficult labor. When he finally did exit his mother's womb, he came out kicking and screaming. Again, the doctor handed me my newborn child to hold, but had yet to wipe him off. I looked down upon my screaming, slimy, infant son and should have known at that moment just how different my two boys would grow up to be. I placed Corey back into my wife's arms, thanked God that he was healthy, and then went to get a strong drink.

As I write my thoughts down while thinking of my sons, I may skip back and forth a bit in time. It's just funny how different things strike you at different times while watching other children play, or looking at old photos, or even watching television. What I truly loved about how my sons both described something was the fact that it was the undiluted version that was spilling from their mouth. They would tell you exactly what they saw, how they saw it and what was on their mind. My first example of this is the time Casey was three and came in from outside. He said, "Daddy, I peed on a tree and washed a bug at the same time." Shortly after Casey had made that statement I had begun to look at bugs much more closely. It was then that I noticed we did have the cleanest bugs in the neighborhood, thanks to Casey's active bladder.

Well, that was funny, but I also noticed that Casey was using the toilet inside less and less, and the great outdoors more and more. Another time he came in from the outside and said in the proudest of voices, "Daddy, if I push on my tummy I can pee way farther." Well, I tried it and came to find out he was absolutely right.

The Last Stand

My oldest son, all of three, and I are at a stand off.
"You will eat your peas or you will not leave this table."
His eyes cold and dark stare back at me. "No!"
He glares at me like a Matador's bull that has been speared,
angry, but hurt.
He speaks softly but deliberate, "I'm not going to eat my peas
and you can't make me."
"No cartoons."
"So."
"No dessert."
"So."
"Santa Clause is watching."
"Nuh uh."
"Son, eat your peas or you'll be sitting here all night."
"I hate peas."
Such powerful language from a three-year-old child!
"Fine then, if you're not going to eat your peas, you are going
to bed."
"I won't eat my peas."
"Off to bed, goodnight."
As he leaves the table he mumbles through his tears, "I hate
peas," and then adds something like, "and my daddy, too."
Why you little brat, I think to myself, and that's when it hits
me… I never eat my peas either!

I guess it is in that three-to-four-years-old range that they become so amused with the control they have over their bladder. When my youngest son, Corey, reached three, he approached his mom one day and said, "Mommy, guess where I am going?"

"I don't know," she said, "where are you going?"

"Pee!"

Trish would always help Corey go to the bathroom and make sure he was clean and washed his hands afterward. She was the bathroom hygienist. Well, one day his brother Casey, who was four, walked up to me and asked "Daddy, why do we sit on our butts?"

I said to him, "Honey, I guess because they are soft and easier to sit on then our heads."

Corey, who was sitting nearby, chimed in, "My mama is the best wiper butt in the world." To this day I bet that Trish is still the best "wiper butt" in the world. Now there's a title a mother can wear with distinction!

As Corey turned four and Casey six years old, it seems like they really bonded as friends. Casey was the leader and Corey would follow anxiously. They became inseparable. I only wish now that they had that same enthusiasm for one another. I know life comes full circle and as they fight like cats and dogs now, I'm confident that as they age they will again begin to grow back together. Best friends for life.

Mentor

Climb, my son of four, up the slide, down and soar.
Teach, my son of six, your brother of four to explore
Those hidden treasures you've found before.
The treasures that wait outside our door
And beckon you both from woods to shore.
Explore, explore, once more, encore!

Children are so funny when it comes to their food—what they like and don't like, how they eat it, how they play with it, how they share it, how they wear it.

I asked Casey if he'd like a bowl of ice cream and he replied, "No."

"Why?" I asked.

"Because I don't like mine cold," he answered.

I think that the last time he had ice cream he ate his too fast and had what we call a "brain freeze," ouch, those things hurt, no wonder he won't eat his ice cream cold anymore. Now, he stirs it until it's soft and soupy. Kids are so quirky about their food.

I was sitting on the couch one day when Casey approached me with a gooey substance all around his mouth. He had eaten about ten jellybeans and was down to the last one. I said, "Casey, will you share your jellybeans with me?"

He said, "Daddy, I only have one left."

"Well then," I said, "can I have that one?"

"No."

He left the room and then came back a moment later. Clearly, his conscious got the better of him. He handed me his last jellybean. Actually, it was the last half of his jellybean, but hey, it's the thought that counts. I ate it with pride!

Ups and Downs

The opposite of high is low,
a wall, the end, nowhere to go.
A snowy field, a lone black crow,
a tag dangling from a junkie's toe.
The opposite of greed is to share,
to hope, to love, to give with care.
A trait in children seldom seen,
oh, thank you precious for half of your jellybean.

A three-year-old child is such a joy to behold. The way they talk and walk, the way they eat their food. Their stature and the way they hold themselves, and, of course, their quirks. God, do they get quirky? It seems like all three-year-olds do something that grabs your attention and makes you laugh without hesitation. Many of them suck their thumb, some carry a blanket or favorite toy around, many just make you smile by the way they cock their head to the side or scratch it as they are trying to understand something. Well, Casey had a quirk that was quite unique. Instead of his thumb Casey would always suck on the two middle fingers of his left hand, while his right index finger rested in his right ear. Every couple of minutes he would pull his right hand from his ear, smell his index finger, then say, "After this I'm going to quit." He would do this throughout the day until he was four years old. A million and one times later after saying, "After this I'm going to quit," later, he did. One day I guess the boy just went cold turkey. After a full year of continuing his little quirk, he just stopped. I only wish I could break some of my bad habits with such confidence. Such will power, I'm so proud of that boy! I must stop bragging. OK, after this I'm going to quit!

Once Casey was done sucking his fingers and sniffing his earwax, he seemed to become slightly more mature over night. I told him he was turning into a big boy one night as he sat on my lap and right away he began talking to me about the aging process. He pointed to my head and asked, "Daddy, what are those two things on your face?"

"Eyebrows," I responded.

"No, not those, these," he said, as he pointed to my forehead.

"Those, Son, are wrinkles."

"Do I have wrinkles?"

"No."

"Why?"

"You're too young, when you get older you will have them."

"Are you old?"

"Yes, honey, I'm an old man. I'm your old man."

"Why am I not old?"

"Because you are young, you will become old in time, Son, be patient."

"Yeah, soon I'll be real old, I'll be five or six." He paused a moment, then said, "You're a real good daddy, even if you are old."

Once I Was Young

When I was young I wished I were old.
A common wish, or so I'm told.
Now I'm old and you are young,
from the fountain of youth it seems you have sprung.
You're the song in my heart, the gleam in my eye.
The reason behind why I laugh and I cry.
One word of advice from your father who's gray.
Hold onto your youth, don't wish it away.

Fairytales, magic, myths, legends—these are all things that make childhood such a wonder. It's often said that innocence is lost when a child stops believing in Santa Claus. Of course, I still believe and my innocence has been long gone. I still get a lump of coal in my stocking every Christmas. How could I not believe?

Taking the boys to the mall to see Santa each year was always one of the highlights of the Christmas season. They would write a list of toys that they hoped to get on a sheet of paper to insure that nothing would be forgotten. One particular year, after we had visited Santa at the mall, Corey was really acting up after we had returned home. Knowing that just an hour earlier he was sitting on Santa's lap telling him how good he had been, Trish decided to remind him of that. "Corey", she said. "What did Santa tell you today?"

Corey became silent for a moment, and then said, "Santa said, Corey, you be a bad boy!"

The little Butt Wipe had an answer for everything, and usually a clever one.

Corey was three at this time and his older brother, Casey, was five, they were born eighteen months apart. So at times as I describe their ages it will seem as if they go from being one year apart to two, but it is dependent upon the month in which I am describing the event. Well, at these particular ages Casey seemed slightly more analytical. He came home from kindergarten one afternoon with the most serious look on his face and began to ask me a series of questions about the authenticity of Santa Claus. He started by saying, "Daddy, there's a girl in our class that doesn't believe in Santa."

"Really," I said.

"I do, though, because how else could boys and girls wake up to toys on Christmas morning?"

"Hmmm, that's a good point," I said. "How else could that happen?"

He paused again, then said, "Daddy, if there really was no such thing as Santa Claus, would the Easter Bunny bring the Christmas presents?"

"Hmmm, let me think about that one for a while, Casey, but I do believe you make a good point." I thought about it all day long with a smile on my face that refused to go away. The Easter Bunny sliding down the chimney, now that's funny! "What's up, Doc, and Merry Christmas to all?"

That year on Christmas morning, Santa, or the Easter Bunny, did arrive. One of the presents that Casey received was a tape of *Beauty and the Beast*. Buying Christmas presents for my boys was so easy back then. Well, Casey watched it twice that day and then asked that we play it again before he went to bed. I said to him as I inserted it into the VCR, "You really love this tape don't you, Casey?"

He said, "Yes, and do you know how long I get to keep it for?"

"No, how long?"

"Forever, or until I die."

"Wow, that's a long time, Casey. Hmmm, sounds like you're going to have that tape for a very long time, Son." I bet he wears it out before he dies! Anyone up for that bet?

Ah yes, the way a child's mind works, so beautifully simple. Who needs logic when you have enough imagination to close your eyes and fly? One day after watching a cute movie about a friendly robot, Casey asked me, "Daddy, where do robots live?"

"They live with whoever builds them," I said.

"So, if Bugs Bunny built a robot then the robot would have to climb down the hole with him to go home."

"Hmmm, I guess. You continue to make good points. Let me think about that one for a while, Son." More pondering, more smiling, more view points to consider. These boys do make me think. Gosh, I think I'm getting a brain freeze!

At five, Casey was beginning to ask some very thought provocative questions and his younger brother was not very far behind.

At three, Casey did the mouth and ear thing with his hands that I have told you about, Corey did the hand in his pants thing. Trish and I would see Corey walking around the house playing with his ding-a-ling and we'd constantly say, "Corey, take your hand out of your pants." One day after reminding him several times to remove his hand from his privates, I said, "Corey, if you keep on playing with that thing it's going to fall off." Now I know I'm not the first parent to say that to their child, but take heed, parents. Why? Because that evening as I was tucking Corey into bed, he said to me, "Daddy, will my peepee really fall off if I keep my hand in my pants?"

"Oh baby, no, of course not, but it is rude to walk around with your hand in your pants."

"Good," he said, "because I've been really worried about that all day and even cried a little."

Poor baby, such trauma at such an early age! In retrospect, I guess I'd cry, too, if I thought mine was going to fall off, even at my age.

It seemed as though a day would never pass when I wouldn't hear something come out of one of my son's mouths that would amuse me for the entire day. That's why I began to record their conversations very early on. Of course there were those days, too, when they would get on a roll and everything they said would crack me up. They both just seemed to continue to grow funnier. As I look back now, I see many similarities between what my two boys said at similar ages in their lives. The best example I have of this is when Casey was six and sitting out in the living room watching television. A preview was showing for an upcoming movie when he yelled from the living room, "Mom, Dad, will one of you take me to see this movie?"

"Sure, what is the name of it?"

"PG 13," he said.

Hmmmm, PG13 and the lad is only six, I thought, as I laughed out loud.

Like deja vu all over again, yes a Yogi ism, when Corey was six the same exact thing occurred. Corey was watching television, a preview of a movie came on in which Corey wanted to see and he asked, "Daddy, will you take me to a movie?"

"Sure, hon, what would you like to see?"

"Coming to theaters everywhere soon."

I guess history really does repeat itself. This one was also rated PG13.

Casey and Corey have even gone through the same styles of dress at the same ages. When Casey was four, he had a baseball cap that he would always wear backward. As Corey became four, he would wear his cap the same way. Honestly, I had no problem with the cap backward, even thought it looked kind of cute. I did, however, have a problem when he began dressing himself and would come from his room with his pants on backward. I would always scoop him up like a bag of potatoes, throw him back on his bed, than proceed to undress and straighten him out. One day I had my hands full when he walked out of his room with his pants on backward. I said, "Corey, your pants are on backwards, go back into your room and turn them around."

He said, "I know they are, but I'll just walk around backwards today."

I told you the boy has an answer for everything. Just between you and I, I know where he gets it from… his mom. Some traits come honest!

Casey's the same way. I got mad at Casey for stepping on bugs one day and he said he wasn't. I said, "Casey, I'm standing here watching you."

"I'm not stepping on them, they're crawling under my shoe," he replied. See what I mean? Do you want to know whom he gets it from? Yep, his mom!

Three

So funny, all the things you say.
So funny, just to watch you play.
So funny, as you reach for hugs.
So funny, as you point at bugs.
So funny, when you laugh at me.
So funny, when you finally see,
why we laugh at you at three. So funny!
You're just so damn funny!

One day Trish and I took the boys to the beach to feed the ducks. We had sprinkled some breadcrumbs out and the ducks were pecking away at them. Out from nowhere came a big goose that was now eating all of the crumbs. Casey yelled out, "Get out of the way, you stupid goose."

Trish said, "Casey, don't call that goose names or she will get mad at you and come bite you."

Talk about me scaring the boys!

Well, some time had passed by and all of the fowl had disappeared, as well as the boys. Trish and I were sitting quietly on the beach enjoying the sunset and the peace and quiet. Suddenly, Corey's cries pierced the silence like a freight train's whistle. He came running from behind some bushes with the goose in hot pursuit and right on his tail. As he was running by us he was yelling through his tears, "Casey said it, Casey said it."

I don't know what he called that poor old goose but that was one wild goose chase I'll never forget. Trish and I truly appreciated the beautiful sunset that evening, but what we appreciated more was the moment Corey learned not to call other living things names. Mother Goose scared the hell out of that little boy and taught him a lesson in manners.

Appreciative Moment

Years from now, when I reflect on the moments that have
passed me by.
I will hear your giggle in every child's laugh.
The giggle that fills the room as I played piggy toes with you.
When you smile back at me as a man, I will still see your
boyish grin, the one I see now.
Yet, when I reflect back, what I will recall most often is that
twinkle of innocence, the one that flickers like a candle in your
eyes right now.
The truthful innocence that would ask me each morning to look
at how tall you have grown overnight.
I'll miss the wonder you showed when learning something new,
when everything is new through the eyes of a three-year-old.
Let me capture you innocence and hold onto it dearly,
at least for now.
For I know it slips through my mind like a sunset melting into
the ocean.
I'm mesmerized by the moment, yet understand that the
moment is passing even as you stand before me now,
a little bit taller than you were last night.

When Casey was four, one of my friends asked if he could participate in his wedding. He wanted Casey to carry the rings up to the altar on a pillow during the ceremony. After much persuasion Casey finally agreed to perform this task. He was outfitted in a gray tuxedo and had his long blond hair combed to the side and back. He was so handsome! I'll never forget the way he looked that day, all two feet, eight inches of him. He had a small stuffed whale he would carry with him, which was a toy that had evolved from the *Free Willie* movie. There he stood all decked out, holding onto his stuffed toy just as nervous as could be. As people passed by many would stop and tell him how cute he looked, prior to the wedding. Once everyone was inside the church, Casey, Corey, Trish and myself, were ushered to the back where Casey would begin his entrance with the rings. I could sense his hesitance as we were instructing him, so I asked him what was on his mind. "Are you scared, Casey?"

He gave his shoulders a shrug and said, "No, not really, I'm just glad it's him and not me that's getting married today."

Everyone turned around as my giggle echoed through the church's corridors. "Me too, Son, me too."

Referencing back to the *Free Willie* movie. When the sequel came out a couple years later I took both Casey and Corey to see it. Both boys adored the movie. One of the last scenes in the movie had the boy trying to save Willie by giving him a sign telling him to jump over a jetty and thus to freedom. At the end of the movie Corey bolted from his seat and began running toward the screen with his hand up in the position the boy had used to signal Willie to jump. As he ran in this position, he was yelling at the top of his lungs, "Free Willie, Free Willie!" The whole theater was laughing at my aspiring actor. It's so easy to recall all of the happy times a child brings to our lives. Yet, there are those times that every parent understands, when you just want to run away from your kid, or give him or her away, at least temporarily. Do you know how tough it is on your sleeping pattern when your child is cutting teeth? The pain, the agony they put us through as they wake us from our slumber all night long crying. Yeah, yeah, I know they are suffering a bit, too. But, this is about me! Damn it, I do need my beauty rest.

All the joys and pleasure I have received while raising my precious little boys, I recognize. However, I'm allowed to flash back to a few times when I felt like sterilization was a pretty good alternative to parenthood. One of those times with both of my sons was when they were just beginning to cut teeth. We would put their pacifier in the freezer so it would be cold and soothing on their gums. During the day they were both pretty tolerable as we could attend to them without much difficulty. At night, well, that was an entirely different story as Trish and I both needed our sleep desperately. Can you relate? Sure you can, any parent can.

Comforting Corey

His scream pierces the night as both parents simultaneously
bolt forward, awakened from their calm.
Their peace, their quiet, their dreams, all shattered by the voice
that echoes down the corridor like an unexpected winter gust
blowing down your neck.
The little angel roars from his cradle
with the ferocity of a lion in hunt.
His cries are loud and sound angry,
but his intentions are simple.
"Rescue me, my parents."
He is cutting teeth; his sleep, too, has been violated.
"Honey, he's awake again."
"I know, I've got ears, do you have legs?"
"You get him, I've got to get up in two hours,
and I need to sleep."
"I got him last time, it's your turn."
Reluctantly, I rise from the bed and walk down the hallway.
To Corey, my footsteps sound like the voice of a long lost
friend promising comfort.
He's standing in his cradle, his cheeks red and wet,
his arms extend as I draw close.
"Where have you been? I've been crying for you."
"My pacifier, your arms, our rocker, at last, comfort."

A new chapter in our lives began when Casey turned five and Corey three. Trish and I dissolved our marriage. There were many factors that led to this unfortunate demise and the majority of them were my fault. Never the less, after a period of mourning, life did move on. The memories of our family collectively, Trish, Casey, Corey and myself, will always be my fondest, always be my saddest. Like Corey tells me still, at eleven years old, "I wish we were still a family." Of course we still are a family, but I know exactly what he means. When we were "a family" we would often have our dinner in the back yard on a picnic bench where cool breezes would blow from a nearby body of water. It was always pleasant and peaceful back there. On one such night as we sat and laughed during dinner, Casey, who was sitting across from me at the time, said, "Daddy, you've got the bluest eyes I've ever seen." Trish laughed and told Casey to remember to tell his girlfriend that when he gets older. Confused, Casey asked, "Tell my girlfriend that Daddy's got the bluest eyes I've ever seen?" I cracked up.

"Sure, Casey," Trish said, "but you might want to say something nice about her eyes, too."

That was our last summer together, our last summer as a family. Now comes the sad part of the book, hopefully the only sad part. I was literally crushed when Trish left. I won't go into the circumstances here, but I would have done anything in the world to make her stay with us. She said I only wanted to "win" her back because of the competitive nature in me. That wasn't true, though. We had grown up together. We had problems, but all marriages do. We had two beautiful sons and the potential for a beautiful life. I knew this and I wanted to hold onto it. I didn't think I could raise my sons alone, and I didn't want to. Trish had her reasons for leaving, but what she was leaving was worth staying and fighting for. To this day, I wish that she would have come back to us and that we would have stayed a family. To this day I am sorry for the things we have not all been able to share together as a family. To this day I wonder, what if?

"From the ashes the soul rises, from the pain the words flow."
—Me. 9/11/94

Mute

Your car is packed and you're ready to leave.
Ready to walk right out of my life,
the same way you entered into it, abruptly.
You stop and turn before you leave me.
Before you leave us.
"I love you," you say softly.
I am frozen in silence.
You turn back, get into your car and you are gone.
I stand alone staring blankly ahead.
My lips quiver, "I love you, too,
I've always loved you."
I stand alone staring blankly.
A single tear hits my shoe.

Trish felt tied down and had a great urge to travel. She aspired to reach new heights in her life and often told me so. This was a dream I had shortly after her departure. To this day I remember it so vividly.

Just a dream

Once upon my dream you were a beautiful white horse.
I climbed upon your back and gripped your mane
As you flew towards the heavens.
We were two different creatures, yet,
we were one in the same as we flew in bliss.
I woke with a jolt, my sheets wet from cold sweat.
As we had flown higher I fell from your back.
You turned to look, but never stopped racing towards the sun.
I fell back to Earth alone, holding onto only your memory.

Trish was afraid of tornadoes and always wanted to be comforted during storms. For the longest time after she left, I would curse storms, suspecting she was seeking comfort in someone else's arms.

Rain

December's days are limited to three
as a new year is ready for center stage.
January is upon us.
I wonder what she shall bear, sunshine and prosperity,
or disillusions and rain?
Last January brought rain,
rain that I blessed each time you pulled me close
to protect you from the thunder.
Yes, the year's at end, January's rain long gone.
You, too, have disappeared.
I hope this January brings sunshine, I need that now.
I prefer not to see rain clouds sweep in from the horizon.
I prefer not to wonder who holds you when they do.
I prefer not to contemplate why rainy days are so sad
and why you're so far away.

One of the reasons I began to collect my sons' thoughts and quotes on paper was to be able to share them with Trish. I knew there would be so many moments in the boys' lives that I wish she were able to witness and wouldn't be able to do so, so I thought I could at least do this for her. Don't I sound like a saint? Believe me when I say I am not. In truthfulness I also wanted her to realize what she was missing as a consequence of her actions. However, once some time passed, the bitterness in me did as well. Now I'm happy that I do have the means to share with Trish what she missed, for all the right reasons. After all, once you have children together you two are joined at the hip for the rest of your lives. Trish will always be my sons' mother and I am grateful.

Well, as the story continues, our three lads are now fending for themselves. Lost, without a female to pick up after them. We now have a situation, which another poem was able to describe much better than myself. It was called "rub-a-dub-dub, three men in a tub." This, my friends is what we were now faced with. All boys under one roof, all chaos all the time, me cooking, cleaning, storytelling, and kicking butt. What a mess! No wonder I cried so hard the day Trish left. I got a brief glimpse into the future.

The first thing I had to face up to was the fact that my boys hated my cooking. I tried so hard to please them but no matter what I cooked they would usually stick their nose up at it. One evening Corey was actually eating something that I cooked and was trying to be polite about it as he made the following statements: "Daddy, when I talk with food in my mouth, I put it back by my cheek so people won't see my icky food—I mean my yummy, chewed up food."

OK, so my cooking is icky. In an effort to please the boys and ease my conscience, as I began to think they were going to die malnourished, I devised a plan. I would let them prepare a menu and I would be able to cook them dinners that they would actually eat, for it was their menu. A win-win situation, right? Well, this was the menu that they came up with after spending about an hour amongst themselves working out the details, a menu that all children could embrace with joy. Surely, a menu for the ages, the young ages that is. This is the menu they handed to me:

Casey and Corey's Menu

Monday-	Macaroni and Cheese
Tuesday-	Fried eggs
Wednesday-	Hotdogs
Thursday-	Pizza
Friday-	Peanut butter sandwiches
Saturday-	Shrimp
Sunday-	We don't want anything

Yep, that's not a typo. On Sunday they wanted no part of my cooking. Well, I guess since the Lord rests on the Sabbath, why shouldn't I? I will do no cooking on Sunday. What I began to do is to take them to a fast food place after church on Sundays. One such day while we were chewing the fat (so to speak), Corey asked, "If we lifted our house up would we see the devil?"

"No," I said.

"Why, is he in the middle of the earth, or is he in the ocean?" He paused briefly then said, "No, that's ridiculous, the devil's too hot for the ocean."

I smiled and said that he should take this discussion back to his Sunday school teacher next week. I'd love to hear their explanation to you on this intriguing subject.

I've jumped off of the subject of cooking here momentarily, but speaking of cooking... One night while I was in the kitchen preparing their meal, Corey came running into the kitchen. He was watching a James Bond film on the television and said, "Daddy, I just saw a bodacious babe. You'd love her! Even I liked her." This, coming from the mouth of a five-year-old. Sunday cannot arrive soon enough. Bodacious babes? I'm not even dating. Help me, Jesus, help me!

Corey gave me the ultimate compliment tonight. He said, "I'd rather have you for my daddy than Sammy Sosa." This, the year that Slammin' Sammy is looking at hitting sixty home runs for the second season in a row. I guess Corey really does love me. It wasn't long after he said that, when he got up to go to the bathroom. When he came back, he sat down, looked at me and said, "Daddy, if I didn't go pee for thirty years, when I finally did go, how long would I pee for?

"Hmmm, Corey, that's a good question. Let me ponder it for a while, but I do bet it wouldn't be thirty years."

When Corey was four, he busted his lip open while playing on the playground just before we were to leave for Florida on vacation. Due to the type of injury and the time frame we would be in Florida, the doctor showed me how to remove the stitches and gave me the instruments to do so. It all sounded so easy at the time—wrong! When the day arrived that I was to remove the stitches, I successfully removed one, but all of the other ones were too deep in the skin and Corey was screaming unmercifully for me to stop. I was at wit's end, as the doctor had told me specifically to remove them by this day or the skin could cover them and cause problems. We were in Florida and I felt helpless, when suddenly I had a brainstorm. Across from the hotel we were staying at was a Veterinarian. Well, what would you have done? The Vet was more than happy to help with my dilemma and removed the remaining stitches with hardly any discomfort on Corey's end. Since that day I've teased Corey about taking him to the Vet and tell him that's why he comes running to me every time I whistle. He'll also chase a ball as long as I keep throwing it. No wonder he's such a great baseball player. I knew I should have stuck with my gut instincts and named him Spike.

March

My boys, together in cadence, march right out the door.
There are so many things new to discover.
There are so many new adventures to be had by them.
I watch from the window, I smile,
I laugh aloud at a gesture made.
My mind photographs the innocence
while my heart grips the moment.
My sons, there are times when I wish that your youth would
never end.
I wish your laughter would echo towards the sun forever,
like this one second in time.
I share at your wonder and marvel at your joy as you march
through the door.
I watch knowing that time stops for no one and marches in
cadence with you.

When Trish and I dissolved our marriage, I decided to relocate. Not a great distance away, only about thirty miles into another county of Maryland. It hurt to see her so often in the same places we would once go to together. Also I was always getting Trish sightings from my friends, who meant well, but didn't realize I didn't need the updates. So, after much searching I found a home, which I thought would be ideal to raise the boys in. It was within walking distance of a beautiful body of water and nestled in the woods on a dead-end street. Very near our home I found a spot, which I truly loved. It was a hill overlooking the river below and was situated perfectly to see the low lying areas and the sun as it set beyond the river. As the sun would set it would spill its warm colors into the mouth of the river. Oranges and pinks would reflect from the water like a painter's pallet spilling colors onto a canvas. I would often take the boys there to watch the sunsets and to sit and talk with them. It was important to me to make sure through their conversations that they were adjusting to our new environment. One afternoon we were driving by the hill just as the sun was setting, so I asked Casey if he would like to stop at our "special spot?"

He asked, "Why is it special?"

"Because we visit it often and make it special to us."

He then asked, "Can we make any place a special spot for us?"

"Sure," I said.

"Then can we make our special spot Kings Dominion?"

"No, but nice try!" What a visionary, surely a sign of things to come.

While I was laughing at him I looked over at Corey, who was eating chocolate ice cream at the time, no, let me rephrase that, he was wearing chocolate ice cream at the time. I said to him, "Corey, you're really making a mess."

To which he replied, "I'm four, how am I supposed to eat this without making a mess?"

"You're not, honey, you're not." How do these kids come up with such great points? I hope they both join the debate teams in high school, now that would be worth paying admission to.

At the ripe old age of four, Corey has been on a roll. His one-liners come with such perfect delivery that you'd swear that he has a group of writers working for him. How could that be? He hasn't even seen Hollywood yet, but I have the feeling that is where he belongs and may end up one of these days. Here are a few examples:

He asked me for a Hershey's Kiss by saying, "Daddy, can I have a Hershey Hug."

"Well, of course you can, honey, but first let me eat your Hershey's Kiss."

His throat was itching and he told me, "There's something stuck in my throat and it feels like a toe nail."

"Well, if it feels like a toenail, it probably is a toe nail. Now how do you think it got their, Corey?"

"Well, I have been chewing my toes lately," he said as he shrugged his shoulders.

In trying to conquer the English language, he asked me, "Does every word mean a word?"

"Well, they're all supposed to mean something, Corey, however, lots of words spoken are spoken without true meaning or much thought put into them." Wow, that sounded so philosophical. Did I say that?

One night as I slept, Corey came into my room and woke me up. I looked at the clock to see that it was three o'clock in the morning. "Is something wrong, baby?" I asked.

"No, what comes after eight hundred and nine?"

"Eight hundred and ten."

"Oh, good night, Daddy."

"Easy for you to say, now I can't sleep!"

Actually, his timing and delivery was way off on that occasion. I NEED MY BEAUTY REST! I could have killed him. I had to start counting Koala bears in order to get back to sleep. Who needs sheep when you can count Koalas? (Koalas are referenced in the following pages, and you'll know where I'm coming from.)

During this time of my life I had dated very infrequently. Mostly, because good baby sitters were hard to come by and expensive. Also, I knew the boys' ability to embarrass the hell out of me without even trying. Here's an example of what they were capable of. I had a date over to the house one evening and she was gracious enough to have cooked dinner for us all. Corey didn't eat much, but when he was finished and my date asked if he had gotten enough to eat, he said, "Yes, I have a full stomach ache, thank you."

Corey, yikes! C'mon lil man, I'm trying to make an impression here... help.

I think that means yes, she said, as she blushed.

"I have a full stomach and mine doesn't even ache," I told her in a feeble attempt to make light of the situation. I'm happy to say it worked. At least for the time being.

Later that same evening, while we were cleaning the icing off of the bowls and spoons from a cake she had baked, Casey said to her, "And just what do you think you are doing? It's a kid's job to lick that stuff off, you know." She was such a nice girl, too. I miss her!

Reach for the stars

Reach for the stars while you're still young,
You have no idea how high they are hung.
Right now they're in reach each night as you play,
Right now they seem close, yet youth fades away.
Soon they'll seem distant like a fond fleeting dream,
It's then I'll remember in your eyes how they'd gleam.
They'll still be in reach and seem close at hand,
But harder to grasp as you grow into a man.

During a short period of time it seemed that Corey would find humor in everything I said. Maybe he should write a book, too? He would always ask me to tell him something funny, and then just crack up. After one such joke he said, "Daddy, stop! You can't make me laugh like this all day, I have a stomach ache." Here all this time I had thought it was from my cooking.

Another time he asked me, "Why do you always come home with funny stuff to say and we don't?"

"Corey, you come home with funny stuff every day of your life, believe me."

He was referring to coming home from kindergarten with jokes. He would hear someone tell a joke and then come home excited and repeat it. One such joke went like this: "Daddy, say I."

"I"

"Now spell cup."

"C-U-P"

He begin to laugh hysterically, as if it were the funniest joke he had ever heard, then said, "Do you get it?"

Jokingly, I said, "No."

His face had a puzzled look on it, and then he said, "I didn't either."

"See, Corey, now that is funny!" He still didn't get it, perhaps now he will?

So funny, these boys of mine are. Casey would always get the mail from the mailbox once he was let off of the school bus. One day he came running in waving a letter excitedly. "Daddy, we got a letter from the President."

"The President?" I asked. "The President of what?"

"The United States I guess."

The letter was labeled, "resident." I told him, "We're only a P away from being important, Son." With that, he went to Pee.

At that time Casey was in the first grade. He had brought home a report that had a smiley face on it from his teacher. Casey handed it to me and said that I should read this, so I did. The paper had been written about a topic they had been discussing in school. The topic was reincarnation. Casey had written, "If I were reincarnated I would like to come back as King Kong. I would like this because I could swing from tree to tree. I could break trees and I could crash camps. I could climb on top of the school. I wouldn't have to brush my teeth. I would not have to take a bath and I would not have to always go pee before I got in the bath tub." He received an "A" and the teacher had written, *very good imagination*. What an understatement, if she only knew.

What is it with kids and brushing their teeth anyway? Why do they all hate to do it? I know I did! Now, my boys do. It's actually work to get them to brush at least twice a day, morning and night. One day I told Corey to get dressed because he was going to go the dentist with me. Reluctantly, he complied. Once we were there we both went back to the dentist chair, where I reclined and the dentist began looking inside of my mouth. Corey then asked the dentist, "Am I next?"

"No," the dentist replied, "just your dad today, Corey."

"You mean I brushed my teeth for nothing," he said.

It's hard to laugh with fingers in your mouth, but I did. The dentist was laughing, too. *Whoa, easy big guy with that drill in your hand. I knew I should have brushed more often when I was a kid.*

Double Your Pleasure

You me laugh, you make me cry.
You me smile and wonder why.
Why I'm blessed with sons of two,
When, after all, just one would do.

Since we're on the topic of double, I've been doing double duties and I'm also receiving double rewards. Corey came up to me recently and said, "Here, Daddy, I made you a Mother's Day card." Of course, I do expect a Father's Day card, too.

Casey recognizes all of the things I do compared to other fathers, who have a spouse. He told me the other day that I was "a real good mom, but even a better dad." That's comforting. Of course, I'm still having problems with the cooking thing. Just can't get those kids to eat. Here on the bay where we live, there is plenty of seafood available. One of the main treats that come from the bay is the Maryland blue crab. In order to catch them you take a chicken neck, tie it to a string, then lower it into the water. The crab will grab the chicken neck with its claws and begin to eat it. You slowly raise the string, pulling the crab towards the surface and then scoop it up with a net. It's easy, fun, and the crabs are delicious. Both of my sons enjoy picking and eating crabs, so we do it often. One day after a day of crabbing we came home with empty buckets. No crabs to eat, so, I fried some chicken for dinner and called the boys in to eat. Casey took one look at the table and promptly responded, "I've seen enough chicken from crabbing today to last me a lifetime, can we please have something else?"

Even though my boys don't eat my food, I still make them sit at the table with me and pick at something before they're excused. If for no other reason, it always makes for animated conversation. One night at dinner Corey looked up from his food and asked, "Daddy, did all of the people who invented food name it themselves, or just the people who have to eat it?"

Hmmm, let me think on it. I sure do give that answer a lot, don't I? One weekend while the boys were at their mother's house I decided to get ahead of the game, so I cooked several meals to serve during the course of the week. I baked a pie, barbecued some spare ribs and chicken, baked a ham and prepared a homemade chicken potpie. When the boys returned, Corey walked into the kitchen and opened the refrigerator door. After inventorying all of the items I had cooked, he said, "Man, Casey, Daddy sure cooked a lot of unhealthy things while we were gone."

The boy doesn't know what healthy food is!

"Well," I said, "you are going to eat all of it tomorrow, now off to bed."

"When is it going to be tomorrow?" Corey asked.

"When I wake you up, why?"

"Because I just love tomorrows, I can't wait." he said.

"Tomorrows come too soon, Son, you'll see!"

Age

Age eases upon us like the ocean's tide easing up the shoreline.
But, unlike the tide there is no retreat.
It's something that is ignored by children,
taken for granted by young adults
and stares back from the mirror at the elderly daily.
One day we are young, the next we are old, or so it seems.
Age is as predictable as the rooster's crow breaking the silence,
Wrinkles breaking the smoothness.
Some of us age gracefully, we all age consistently.
It's yesterday's memories and today's routines.
It's tomorrow's dreams wrapped with a bow just waiting to be opened.

Corey asked, "Do you remember?"

"Do I remember what, hon?"

"Do you remember the time you shut Casey's door with his lights out and you tried to scare him?"

"Hmmm, I think I do remember doing that, hon, wasn't that yesterday?"

"Yes, I just wanted to see if you remembered it?"

I'm only forty and my boys are already testing me for Alzheimer.

On Saturdays it is usually cleaning time at the old bachelor pad. As I was busy doing the chores Corey said, "I don't want to grow up, you have to work too hard."

Casey, who was standing nearby said, "Not me, I'm just going to lay back in my Jacuzzi and let my kids do the work."

"Casey," I said, "I think you're on to something here. Grab this broom while I lay back."

Corey said, "Daddy, I love you, especially on Saturday."

There's someone who's not going to have to work today. "Casey, grab that mop, too!"

One Saturday after doing the chores I took both of the boys fishing. After many unsuccessful tries at pulling a fish in, Corey asked, "Daddy, if all the people in the world were gone, would there still be fish here?"

"I don't see why not, but why do you ask?"

"Because I don't know who would feed them worms if we didn't."

All right, I admit I am not the greatest fisherman ever to cast a rod, but I have caught a fish before, I swear. I had to take two pictures of it just to show the length of it. I wish I still had the pictures.

At our house I usually have to force the boys to take a bath or shower. After fishing, Corey asked if he could take a bath now, he thought that he was smelling, rather fishy. Still, this was very unusual and I was certainly surprised by the question. "Sure," I said, "run the water and do you need a towel?"

"No."

"Sure you do," I said, "you'll be cold when you get out wet."

"That's OK, I am always cold." He gave me a smile and a wink. I smiled back at him and he asked me, "How do you do that?"

"Do what?"

"Smile like that?"

"Like what?"

"So handsome."

"It's just the love I have for you coming through, Son," and that is the truth. I just love the way my sons look upon me. If only the bodacious babes could see me through their eyes I would certainly have it made as a single man.

The world's Your Playground

I watch as you run through fields of tall golden wheat.
Your giggles dance on the wind and rustle through the tall
strands of grass.
I watch in admiration as you turn nature into your own personal
playground.
I watch and I try to hold onto the sounds of your laughter,
the smells of autumn, the images of your youth as they smile
before me.
As I stand still, the sounds ring through my ears, the fragrance
through my nostrils, the sight of you emblazoned upon my
mind.
The images of youth, the images of love,
the images of the moment.
The images, which will unfold again in the calm of a dream
and the face of a child pressed to my lips.

I took my sons to California in July for our vacation. A girl that I was currently dating came along with us. She had a sister, Rachel, who lived in L.A. We planned on staying with her for a couple of days, prior to driving down to San Diego. One evening while we were staying at Rachel's apartment, she had scheduled to go out on a date. She went to her room to get ready, and then came out about a half an hour later. When she came out of her room Corey looked at her and said, "Wow, you look different. You should go look at yourself in the mirror."

Laughing, I said, "Yeah, Rachel, have you seen yourself lately? You've turned from a caterpillar into a butterfly." Another time while still in L.A. we all got up early and went out for breakfast. The grown-ups ordered the buffet and when the waitress stopped by our table to ask how every thing was, Casey said, "You have the best breakfast in the world here." He had ordered Corn Flakes. I asked Casey how come they were so much better here than they were at home and he replied, "I dunno, maybe it's this California sunshine." Maybe, Casey, it's your imagination!

We had lots of discussions during our drive along the coast. One of the topics that came up was a question asked to the boys. What do you want to be when you grow up? After much deliberation Corey finally spoke up and said, "I'm going to be an athlete, a coach, a sportswriter, or work at Wal-Mart."

I said, "Corey, I think you have a great shot at being the next great greeter at Wal-Mart." Now there's a dream to aspire to.

Another time while still driving the coastline, I had a bad taste in my mouth and rolled down the window to spit. After doing so Corey said, "Dad, when are you going to teach me to spit like you, I can't do it that cool?"

"Well, my son, it really does take years of practice to be able to do it while driving and not have it blow back in your face. We'll start by teaching you on ground level. Once you have the hang of that we'll go to the baseball field and work on your spit ball."

"Cool," he said.

We were very near San Diego when Corey began talking once again about growing up and what he was going to be. He got quiet for a minute then said, "Actually I don't even want to grow up, I love being a kid."

I said, "You should enjoy your youth, it will be gone before you know it and you'll look back to it with fond memories."

He then replied, "Well, the only reason I don't want to be a man is because I don't want to be hairy and smelly."

"Oh." I wonder what he's trying to tell me? I have been driving for sometime now.

My sons growing up, is a thought I continually struggle with. I just want to protect them from everything forever. It's so hard to let go, yet as you watch them grow right before your very eyes you realize they'll be gone in no time. I am continually preparing myself for the day that will happen. It's one reason I truly do enjoy every minute I'm around them. There have been brief moments when for selfish reasons I wished them on their mom, but that was only after she had left the country and I had them twenty four hours a day, seven days a week. Those moments are rare. I am so very lucky and blessed.

Go Quietly

Go now, my son, as quietly as the day you entered into my life.
I've rehearsed this farewell a million times now.
I'm strong, maybe?
I've imagined you leaving by bus, on planes and by foot,
but always leaving.
I've imagined watching you go off to school, off to war,
off to love and just—off.
I've thought about this moment the moment I laid eyes upon
you.
As you turned two, I missed my baby.
As you turned four, I missed my toddler.
As you turned before my eyes,
I couldn't wait to see what you'd turn into.
Always knowing it would be wonderful,
forever missing the moments you left behind.
So, just go, Son.
Go with a smile and go with confidence.
Those attributes will sustain you. I've taught you that.
Go, knowing the love we've shared will only grow stronger,
even in your absence.
Go, knowing that dad will be all right;
I've rehearsed this a million times before.
I'm strong, maybe?

Casey was trying to find his friend's phone number one night and ended up calling information to find it. The operator asked for the city and state and then asked for the listing. Casey replied, "resident."

"No, the name of the resident," the operator asked.

"Farrell," replied Casey.

"Do you know the first name?"

"No, but his two sons are named Kyle and Jimmy."

Well, if he can't find that listing now he should lose his job. I'm still laughing as I think about that conversation.

Corey has a terrible time pronouncing his R's. For example when he tries to say shore, it sounds more like showeh. Today he asked me why we named him what we did and the conversation sounded like this: "Daddy, why did you and mom have to name me Cowey (Corey)? You know I can't pronounce it right. I can say Kevin and Casey fine, but no, you had to name me Cowey. Now, every time someone asks my name I say Cowey, and they say what? So I say Cowey again. Then they say, Cowey? I say no and spell it C-O-R-E-Y, Cowey! Then they finally say, oh, Corey!"

Sorry, Son, how about we give you a nickname, do you like Spike?

He is scheduled to begin working with a speech therapist at school next year. I'm sure it will all "wook out wight for him."

My sister, Cindy, was visiting us one summer and was preparing spaghetti in the kitchen when Corey popped his head around the corner and asked her what she was cooking. "Spaghetti," she said.

"I don't like spaghetti," Corey said back to her.

"Oh, you'll like mine. I make the best spaghetti in the whole world."

"Yeah wight, and I'm Al Gowa." (Yeah right, and I'm Al Gore)
She cracked up. Me too!

As part of his sixth grade fundraiser this year, he asked if I'd
drive him to an exclusive subdivision to sell his products. "Sure,"
I said. Well the day before, we had gone to the county fair and he
had won some big, gaudy, silver plated chains to wear around his
neck like the pop artists do. One had a huge dollar sign hanging
from it and another one had the superman emblem on it. They are
both so big I'm surprised he can even hold his head up straight,
much less walk with them on, but to him they are very cool. Well,
as we got to the subdivision and I let him out, he took a few steps,
stopped, and then came running back to the car. "What is wrong?"
I asked.

"I almost forgot," he said, as he took the chains off his neck
and handed them to me. "You've got to hold my ice or else these
people are going to think I'm a little rich kid and not feel sorry
for me and buy something."

I could only think to myself, *oh I don't think you have to worry
about that*, as I put the junk in the glove box. With holes in his
pants, he turned and went to sell some wares.

Casey and Corey are always talking about homeless people
and saying what they should be doing, such as, sitting in a bus
station during the winter to keep warm. Well, recently both of
them have taken a liking to "Ragoon noodles," which come in a
cup and you just add warm water to turn into a meal. At the store
as I grabbed a few of them Casey noticed the sale sign which said
you could buy a case of fifty Ragoons for six dollars. "Wow," he
said, "This is a homeless man's dream. He could eat healthy for a
month, just add water and dinner is served for only pennies a
day."

"Yeah, Casey, why do you think we eat them so often?" I don't know which one of them says the funniest things, but I do know they both crack me up. I'll never forget the time Casey was five and saw a K-9 police car go by us with a police dog in the back. He promptly asked me, "Daddy, how come the policeman arrested that dog?"

Trying to hold back my laughter, I replied, "I don't know for sure, Casey, but I bet he tried to steal a bone."

Casey paused for a couple of minutes then finally said, "Yeah, that makes sense."

I share these stories with my sons all the time now that they are old enough to recognize the humor. One night Corey lay in bed with me I was telling him some of the things he did and said as a baby. He listened and smiled, then said, "Daddy, I sure wish I could remember all of my memories."

Kevin Clark

I Promised You the Moon

The moon was at hand tonight as the boys insisted we chase it,
follow its beam until we could stand directly under it
and adore it.
As we drove the country roads, it danced through the leaves
like a firefly flickering just beyond a child's reach.
Across the bay it shimmered against the waves like a skimming
stone in search of its last wave.
Over the fields of grain the moon illuminated the soft sway of
golden wheat, as the deer stood mesmerized.
We drove and drove and drove, as the moon mocked us.
Always just beyond us, always just out of reach.
I promised my boys the moon on that September night,
what they found was a pocket full of memories.
Perhaps one day, many moons from now, they, too, will chase a
moonbeam with their children.
Perhaps they'll even catch it.

We were driving down in the city today and on my left was a construction site where a new motel was being built. Casey looked over at it and said, "That's a bad place to put a motel."

Surprised by his observation I asked, "Why do you say that, Casey?"

He responded by saying, "Why would anyone want to stay there? Look at all the dirt and tractors they have to look at all day and I don't even see a pool."

"Well I will certainly make sure that we never stay at that motel, Casey!"

As I'm in my forty's now and look back at my childhood days, it is so ironic that I see the similarities of my children's dreams that seem to mirror my own. I know that we live vicariously through our children and many of the traits, gestures, likes and dislikes are all directly related to the influence that we have on them. Still, it's almost eerie as you see yourself through your child so often as you watch them play a game, or solve a puzzle on their own. I'm often envious as I watch them have so much fun and wish that I could somehow lose whatever grown-up hang-ups that have saddled me along my journey to where I am today. I try very hard to emphasize to my sons that the moments they are enjoying now will be some of the best memories they'll ever have (even if Corey can't remember all of his memories). I believe they'll have a wonderful life, as I have had, but will one day look back, like I often do, and realize that those were the good old days. They'll realize daddy was one hundred percent right, at least about that.

Days, Dreams, Children and Sand

Take me back to childhood days and castles in the sand,
when I could find security in holding Daddy's hand.
Where dreams once loomed as large as stars
and just as far away,
and all I had to think about was one more sunny day.
Funny how the seasons change from boyhood unto man,
and dreams can somehow wash away like castles in the sand.
Sunny days don't seem as bright with each new passing year,
and ocean's salt has turned into the salt found in a tear.
Take me back to childhood days on pastures green and grand,
when I could find security by holding Daddy's hand.
My heroes all wore cowboy boots, on horses they would ride
and stars shone bright into the night with Daddy by my side.
Funny how the seasons change from boyhood unto man,
trees die slow and buildings grow on what was fertile land.
Now heroes come in boxes from the wars year after year,
and security is all but lost in one salt laden tear.
Now, my hands are held by two sons growing straight and tall,
my life has come full circle since my daddy died last fall.
Perhaps one day upon a star, my boys will think of me
and know how much I loved them like my castles by the sea.

Casey, Corey and myself were sitting in the gloom of the evening as a thunderstorm rolled in. We watched the lightning with fascination and listened as the thunder echoed through the woods. Both boys were wide eyed and watching with intensity as I reached over and pinched Corey's butt just as another flash of lightning occurred. Corey just about jumped out of his britches. "Got you," I said, laughing.

"You didn't scare me, I'm allergic to that," he replied. Guess I'll have to take him to the doctor and see if we can't get him something for those allergies.

I swear at times I just can't imagine what goes on in my sons' minds. Even as I am talking to them, their ideas seem so abstract that I can't figure where they're drawing their conclusions from. Never the less, it sure is fun listening to them talk, while I'm scratching my head from their statements and trying to figure things out for myself. A lot of the best conversations seem to occur late at night when the boys are ready for bed. Not all the time, but sometimes they will ask if they can both sleep with me. I rarely say no, as I know this won't last forever either and I want to enjoy their bedtime conversations for as long as I can. One such conversation unfolded like this, as the three of us lay on our backs talking to one another. Corey began the conversation after we had said goodnight to one another by saying, "I wish I lived on a continent."

Casey then said, "You do live on a continent, North America."

To which Corey replied, "Well, I wish I lived at the tip of Brazil because it would always be snowing there."

"It doesn't snow in Brazil," I said to Corey, "it's hot in Brazil."

"I still wish I lived there," he said.

Then Casey said, "I wish I lived in Australia."

"Australia, why there?" I asked.

"So that every morning I could go outside and catch me a Koala Bear. I'd start me a Koala Bear collection."

"Yeah, me too," Corey said.

"Go to sleep, boys, start counting Koala Bears."

I think I'll take them to the zoo the next free weekend we have.

Typical Day

You walk, you run, you laugh and play.
You cry, complain and moan all day.
You're up; you're down, then level out.
I mostly laugh, but often shout.

One morning before school I was getting the boys' breakfast ready. Corey asked, "Daddy, when you make our cereal do you add the cereal to the bowl and then the milk, or do you pour the milk in first?"

Casey spoke up saying, "It's my way to have Daddy pour the cereal into the bowl and then add the milk, it's real good that way."

To which Corey replied, "Yeah, that does sound good. Daddy, make mine like Casey's." Naturally I then proceeded to pour the milk in the bowl first before adding the cereal. To my astonishment they could not tell the difference. I'm just happy they're starting to like my cooking.

Corey was sprucing himself up in the mirror one night after he had gotten out of the bathtub. He was in sixth grade at school and many of the boys had begun using mousse in their hair to make it shiny and stick up. Corey had washed his hair and was now applying the mousse. As he carefully admired his new hair-do he said, "My hair's so shiny and smells so good, this is the goodest thing I've ever done for myself." He did look dashing, I thought. Perhaps that was the *goodest* thing he'd ever done.

My mom comes to visit us quite frequently, even though she lives out of state. We were expecting her one weekend and the boys were talking about her age. She is sixty-five, but could easily pass for fifty. Anyway, Casey was saying to Corey, "I think Nanny will live to be a hundred years old."

To which Corey responded back by saying, "If she lives that long she'll start to look like a grandma." *I sure hope I don't start to look like a granddad until I turn a hundred years old!*

Speaking of age, I look terrible if I don't shave because my whiskers are uneven and many of them gray. One morning as I awoke to find Corey in my bed, I had a two-day growth working from the weekend. I guess this was the first time that Corey had seen me with whiskers because he asked me, with the most peculiar look on his face, "Daddy how'd you get all those splinters on your face?" Once he realized they were whiskers he couldn't stop laughing. Of course, I, too, often laugh when I look at myself in the mirror.

Like I said earlier, when Corey gets on a roll you need to keep your ears open because he says and asks the funniest things.

After I had shown Corey how to shave and we had eaten our breakfast, I was cleaning up the mess. I was pouring the bacon grease from the skillet into a can, when Corey asked, "Daddy, is that oil your pouring into that can?"

I said, "Yes."

To which he replied, "And then you just pour it into your car?"

I said, "Not exactly, Corey."

He shrugged, said, "Oh," and walked away.

We still have the whole day ahead of us. Something tells me this is going to be a good one, and I wasn't wrong. Later that day as we were running some errands together, Corey asked me, "If I were this little and had a baby, but knew how to drive, would you let me take him somewhere?"

I told him that first off, if he had a baby, then I would be a granddad and that I'm too young to be one of those and secondly, if that were to happen he'd have to get his own car because I'm always using mine.

"That's what I thought you'd say," he said.

Funny how he knows my answers before I give them.

The Core Man

The moon twinkles off of your nose like a fairy dancing on a
drop of water.
Your eyes, like the moon, are big and bright,
illuminating your innocence.
The wonderment you show at five is as smooth and refreshing
as your skin.
Do you know that I think about you all day?
I so anticipate your inquisitions,
such as why do I prefer fried over scrambled eggs?
I love to watch you run from the bathtub still soapy,
as you insist you are dry.
I love the way you spring from beneath the water with your
eyes opened wider than a river's mouth.
You're so unique, so special!
Your defiance and rebellious nature are as strong as your
lovingness.
Your butterfly kisses tickle my cheek and make me laugh as
hard as I do when you tell me a joke, and then ask me if I got it,
because you didn't.
You're like an untapped treasure that I want to share with the
world, because I know the world will benefit from your
presence.
The Core man, the core of my soul and what life is all about.
You are joy and happiness in its truest sense, I hope you never
cry from sorrow, but if you do I know that heaven weeps with
you, just as it waits for you.

The Case Man

Your giggles have bounced through my mind like music made
on a warm summer night
since the day I heard your first giggle.
Your voice and your head a tilt, as you ask why I love you,
freeze me like a snow man surrounded by children,
a frozen smile never disappearing.
You're the Case Man, the first born,
my first experience with unconditional love.
I've loved you as you slept, as you grew, as you pouted,
as you played with your piggy toes before going to sleep.
You'll always be the light in a darkened room,
the warmth on a winter day,
the sound of the breeze on a day grown still.
You'll always be my son and I'll always love you,
Just as I promised, for forever and a day.

Corey and I were talking about romance, when he said, "I'm not going to kiss a girl until the day that I get married."

Curious as to why he would wait so long before kissing a girl, I bit, "Why are you going to wait that long?" I asked.

"Because I want to," he said, "and I wouldn't even kiss her then except for the priest makes you when he says, now kiss the bride!"

"Oh, yes you are right, Corey,. I think that's the first time I ever kissed a girl, too."

The next thing I know, Corey's asking me about naming his children once he is married and has them. He asked me, "Can I name my baby anything I want to?"

"Sure."

"You mean that I can name him Mickey or Eric?" (Guess he's planning on a boy.)

"Sure, anything you want, as long as your wife agrees, but why are you asking me?"

"Because I thought only you could name my kid, I didn't know I could, I'd better start thinking of a good name now."

Laughing, I said to him, "Just remember to give him a name he can pronounce. Don't do what I did to you and name him Cowey Junya!"

He said, "Oh, don't worry, I wouldn't do that to the poor kid."

Again, I am Corey's favorite dad. He asked me "Can I stay up as late as I want tonight?"

"Yes," I said.

"Thanks, you're my favorite dad on Friday's." Hmmm, I wonder who is his favorite dad the other six days of the week?

Casey is starting to get into liking rap music now. As I listen to the lyrics I can't help but go back in my mind to the day he approached me and asked, "Daddy, where does Raffi come up with all of those great songs?" We've gone from Raffi to Eminem, in the course of six years. I can only wonder what will come next. Ah yes, the puberty years. Casey is now there and Corey is wondering what is taking him so long.

As we were watching television one night, Corey said, "Daddy, did you know Casey has a patch of hair on his privates now?"

"Uh, no, I wasn't aware of that, but actually it doesn't surprise me," I said back to him.

"He'll show it to you if you ask him, he's real proud of it."

"Uh, no thanks, Corey."

I guess I have in the making the sequel to this book: *The Puberty Years*. What do you think? I'm sure I will have a lot more to write about.

Hey Boys

I love you more than pudding and rice,
because in you both is all that is nice.
And good in a world I enter each day,
and return home to you, each night I pray.
You're my sons, the two I hold in my heart,
and look in your eyes each day as I start.
And as each day ends and another begins,
I'm so very grateful for you guys and friends.

Corey is still my cuddle bug at age 12. He doesn't like to cuddle quite as often as he did a couple of years ago, never the less, it is often that he asks if he can snuggle up with me while watching television on the couch. As I wrap my arms around him, he often holds my arm and caresses my hands saying how much he likes them. He says he likes the feel and the size and the strength he feels when he touches them. I love knowing that he feels this way.

Hands

"I love your hands."
"Because they are pretty?"
"I love your hands."
"Because they are strong?"
"I love your hands."
"Because they are supportive?"
"I love your hands."
"Because they massage?"
"I love your hands."
"Because they hold you?"
"I love your hands."
"I know you do, Corey, because they stretch across your back
on nights, so cool,
Across your hands when going to school.
Across your brow when you're not cool,
Across your mouth if you act the fool."
"I love your hands."
"Son, I love having you in my hands!"

As I close my eyes and think back to the days when butterfly kisses and giggles met me at the door each day as I arrived home from work, I realize how precious each day of our lives is. One thing that I hope I can instill upon my sons is that the gift of love is the greatest gift of all. I have always told them that I love them for forever and a day, as forever never seemed long enough to encapsulate how long I will love them for. Today, I am so grateful for today because I love and am loved in return. Don't miss the opportunity to tell those you love, "I love you," now, today. Don't wait a minute longer. Tomorrow comes too fast and forever is not quite long enough, but today is yours. Embrace it!

Printed in the United States
23174LVS00001B/278

9 781413 747126